BLAZERS®

X GAMES

Snowboarder X

Reading Consultant:
Barbara J. Fox
Reading Specialist
North Carolina State University

Content Consultant:
Ben Hobson
Content Coordinator
Extreme Sports Channel
United Kingdom

Capstone
press
Mankato, Minnesota

Blazers is published by Capstone Press,
151 Good Counsel Drive, P.O. Box 669, Mankato, Minnesota 56002.
www.capstonepress.com

Library of Congress Cataloging-in-Publication Data
Miller, Connie Colwell, 1976–
    Snowboarder X / by Connie Colwell Miller.
    p. cm.—(Blazers. X games)
    Includes bibliographical references and index.
    ISBN-13: 978-1-4296-0111-5 (hardcover)
    ISBN-10: 1-4296-0111-6 (hardcover)
    1. Snowboarding—Juvenile literature. 2. ESPN X-Games—Juvenile
literature. I. Title. II. Series.
GV857.S57M544 2008
796.939—dc22   2007001744

Summary: Describes the sport of snowboardercross, focusing on the X Games,
    including competitions and star athletes.

Essential content terms are bold and are defined at the bottom of the page where they first appear.

Editorial Credits
Mandy R. Robbins, editor; Bobbi J. Wyss, designer; Jo Miller, photo researcher

Photo Credits
AP/Wide World Photos/Keystone, Arno Balzarini, 27; Nathan Bilow, 6, 7 (both)
Corbis/Duomo, 12, 19; epa/Franco Debernardi, 14
Getty Images Inc./Bongarts, 22–23; Brian Bahr, cover; Doug Pensinger, 4–5, 8
WireImage/E. Bakke, 11, 13, 16–17, 28¬–29; Garrett Ellwood, 20
ZUMA Press/Justin Kase Condor, 15; K.C. Alfred/SDU-T, 26; Norbert Falco/
    Maxppp, 24–25; Tony Donaldson/Icon SMI, 21

1 2 3 4 5 6 12 11 10 09 08 07

Table Of Contents

Second Chance

In January 2007, X Games fans crowded the slopes near Aspen, Colorado. The women's snowboarder X (SBX) competition was in full swing. Lindsey Jacobellis led the riders down the **course**.

course (KORSS)–a set path; SBX riders compete on a course set on a mountainside.

Jacobellis had wiped out at the 2006 Winter Olympics, and it cost her the gold medal. This was her second chance. Joanie Anderson was in second place. But that changed on the last jump, when Jacobellis landed too far forward.

Joanie Anderson

She tumbled awkwardly to the finish line. Joanie Anderson sped past her and won the race. SBX fans thought they knew who would win the race. They were wrong.

SBX Basics

In SBX, six riders race down a steep course. They carve around sharp turns and sail over icy jumps.

berm

SBX got its name from motocross.
Both sports have courses with jumps,
turns, and **berms**. SBX has also been
compared to NASCAR for its fast pace
and many crashes.

**berm (BURM)—a banked turn
or corner on an SBX course**

BLAZER FACT

SBX became part of the Winter Olympics in 2006.

SBX riders try to stay in control while speeding through the course. Riders often collide or wipe out. The first boarder to cross the finish line in the final race wins.

Competing in SBX

In SBX competitions, riders get two **qualifying** runs. Riders who qualify compete in groups of six. The top three riders in each group advance.

qualify (KWAHL-uh-fye)—to earn a spot in the main event by competing well in early races

The six fastest riders compete in the final round. Unlike other snowboarding competitions, SBX winners are decided by a clock—not a judge.

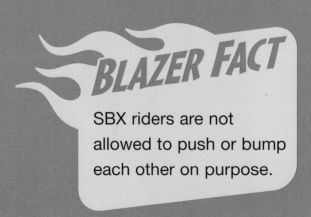

BLAZER FACT

SBX riders are not allowed to push or bump each other on purpose.

Most riders love snowboarding
so much that they would race for free.
But SBX winners also earn cash and
prizes worth thousands of dollars.

SBX Course Diagram

finish line

jump

SBX All Stars

Seth Wescott was the first U.S. rider to win an Olympic medal in SBX. Wescott also took first place at the X Games seven times.

American Lindsey Jacobellis leads the pack in women's SBX. She has won three gold medals at the X Games.

Lindsey Jacobellis

Riders like Wescott and Jacobellis are blazing the way in SBX. Fans can expect faster, more exciting races as the sport grows in popularity.

Taking off down the slope!

Glossary

berm (BURM)—a banked turn or corner on a SBX course

competition (kom-puh-TISH-uhn)—a contest

course (KORSS)—a set path; SBX riders compete on a course.

jump (JUHMP)—a built-up area of snow that SBX riders jump over

motocross (MOH-toh-kross)—a sport in which people race motorcycles on dirt tracks

qualify (KWAHL-uh-fye)—to earn a spot in the main event by competing well in early races

Read More

Kalman, Bobbie, and Kelley MacAulay. *Extreme Snowboarding*. Extreme Sports No Limits. New York: Crabtree, 2004.

Doeden, Matt. *Shaun White*. Amazing Athletes. Minneapolis: Lerner, 2007.

Internet Sites

FactHound offers a safe, fun way to find Internet sites related to this book. All of the sites on FactHound have been researched by our staff.

Here's how:
1. Visit *www.facthound.com*
2. Choose your grade level.
3. Type in this special code **1429601116** for age-appropriate sites. You may also browse subjects by clicking on letters, or by clicking on pictures or words.
4. Click on the **Fetch It** button.

FactHound will fetch the best sites for you!

Index